Inside the Military

MILITARY AIRCRAFT

DiscoverRoo
An Imprint of Pop!
popbooksonline.com

Emma Bassier

abdobooks.com

Published by Pop!, a division of ABDO, PO Box 398166,
Minneapolis, Minnesota 55439. Copyright © 2020 by POP,
LLC. International copyrights reserved in all countries. No
part of this book may be reproduced in any form without
written permission from the publisher. Pop!™ is a trademark
and logo of POP, LLC.

Printed in the United States of America, North Mankato,
Minnesota.

052019
092019

THIS BOOK CONTAINS
RECYCLED MATERIALS

Cover Photo: US Department of Defense
Interior Photos: US Department of Defense, 1, 25, 31 (right);
US Air Force, 5, 6, 8–9, 11, 14–15, 16 (top), 16 (bottom), 17
(top), 19, 21, 30; US Navy, 7, 20, 23 (bottom), 26, 29; Library
of Congress, 12, 13; Defense Visual Information Distribution
Service, 17 (bottom), 22, 27; iStockphoto, 23 (top left), 23
(top right), 31 (left); Shutterstock Images, 28

Editor: Connor Stratton
Series Designer: Jake Slavik
Library of Congress Control Number: 2018964853
Publisher's Cataloging-in-Publication Data
Names: Bassier, Emma, author.
Title: Military aircraft / by Emma Bassier.
Description: Minneapolis, Minnesota : Pop!, 2020 | Series:
    Inside the military | Includes online resources and index.
Identifiers: ISBN 9781532163821 (lib. bdg.) | ISBN
    9781644940556 (pbk.) | ISBN 9781532165269 (ebook)
Subjects: LCSH: Military airplanes--Juvenile literature. |
    Military helicopters--Juvenile literature. | Military
    vehicles--Juvenile literature.
Classification: DDC 623.746--dc23

WELCOME TO
DiscoverRoo!

Pop open this book and you'll find QR codes loaded

with information, so you can learn even more!

Scan this code* and others

like it while you read, or visit

the website below to make

this book pop!

popbooksonline.com/military-aircraft

*Scanning QR codes requires a web-enabled smart device with a QR code reader app and a camera.

TABLE OF
CONTENTS

CHAPTER 1
FIGHTERS

A **pilot** flies his airplane through the sky. He checks his **radar** for enemy planes nearby. His plane could fire **missiles** or its machine gun at them. The gun shoots many bullets quickly.

WATCH A VIDEO HERE!

A US fighter pilot fires a missile.

Fighters are a type of military airplane. They are mainly built to attack other planes in the air. Fighters have powerful engines. These engines allow fighters to increase their speed quickly.

 **DID YOU KNOW?** Most modern fighters can fly faster than the speed of sound.

A fighter traveling faster than sound achieves supersonic speed.

Fighters also have large wings.

Their large wings and strong engines help

pilots turn quickly without slowing down.

A US fighter pilot shows off the plane's speed.

This ability helps them deal with other planes. Today, fighters are also built to deal with enemies on the ground.

CHAPTER 2
HISTORY OF MILITARY AIRCRAFT

Militaries first used airplanes in the early 1900s. These airplanes were for **reconnaissance**. From high above, **pilots** gathered information about their enemies. For example, pilots could learn

LEARN MORE HERE!

The first military airplane prepares for flight.

their enemy's location. This information

helped military leaders with their plans.

The first military airplane was a Wright Model A made in 1909.

In the 1910s, militaries built airplanes for fighting. These early fighters had machine guns. During this time, most early airplanes had two sets of wings. They also had **propellers**. These planes could not fly very quickly. And they could not carry much weight.

Airplanes with two sets of wings are called biplanes.

Militaries first used jet engines on a large scale during World War II (1939–1945).

By the 1940s, most military airplanes had one set of wings. Planes also started using jet engines instead of propellers. These advances made planes faster. Planes could also carry more weight.

U.S AIR FORCE
O-14120

MILITARY AIRPLANES
TIMELINE

1925

Max speed:
140 miles per hour

1941

Max speed:
440 miles per hour

1945

Max speed:
580 miles per hour

2018

Max speed:
1,200 miles per hour

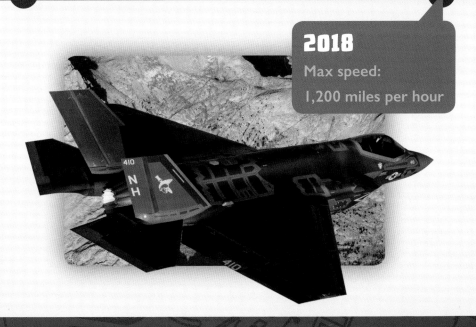

CHAPTER 3
BOMBERS

Bombers are another type of military airplane. Militaries use bombers to attack buildings and people on the ground. These planes carry heavy loads, such as bombs and **missiles**.

LEARN MORE HERE!

A B-52 bomber leads a group of US fighters.

Bombers are the largest type of military aircraft. Their size makes them easy to attack. For this reason, some bombers are built to avoid **radar**. Radar is a system that sends out radio signals.

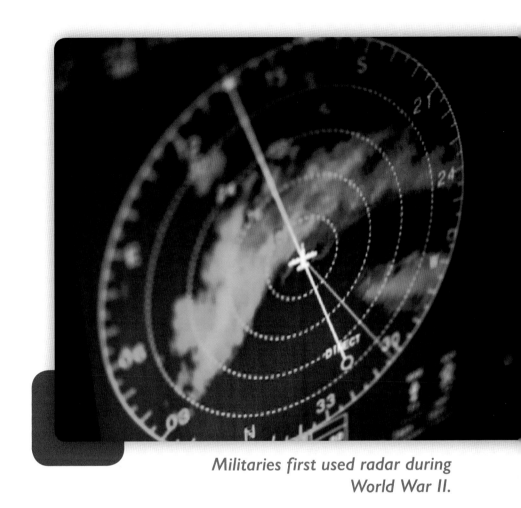

Militaries first used radar during World War II.

These signals bounce off objects and return to the radar system. Then, the system can learn where the objects are.

To escape radar, bombers have curved surfaces. This shape causes signals to bounce in other directions. Bombers' surfaces soak up many signals too. The signals do not bounce back. So, the radar system cannot see the bomber.

Bombers built to avoid radar are often called stealth bombers.

HOW RADAR WORKS

Radar depends on satellites. A satellite sends out a radio signal. The signal bounces off a plane and returns to the satellite. The signal shows up on the radar screen. A soldier can see the plane's location.

satellite

radio signal

enemy plane

radar screen

CHAPTER 4
HELICOPTERS

Militaries first used helicopters in battle in the 1950s. Helicopters have many different uses. They take soldiers from one place to another. These aircraft deliver weapons and supplies to soldiers.

COMPLETE AN ACTIVITY HERE!

US Army helicopters practice transporting weapons.

Helicopters help with **reconnaissance**

as well. They can also attack enemies.

Helicopters can hover in place with the help of their two rotors.

A helicopter uses **rotors** to fly.

A rotor is similar to a **propeller**.

One rotor is on top of the helicopter.

The other rotor is on its tail. These two rotors let helicopters go where airplanes cannot.

The US Navy uses certain helicopters to deal with enemy submarines. These helicopters fly close to the water. Then, they lower **sonar** devices into the water. Sonar is similar to **radar**. Helicopters use sonar to see if any submarines are nearby.

A US Navy helicopter drops a sonar device into the water.

MAKING CONNECTIONS

TEXT-TO-SELF

Would you rather fly a fighter, a bomber, or a helicopter? Why?

TEXT-TO-TEXT

Have you read books about other kinds of aircraft? How are they similar to and different from military aircraft?

TEXT-TO-WORLD

Military aircraft have powerful weapons. What should pilots think about before using those weapons?

GLOSSARY

missile – a weapon that is fired at a target.

pilot – a person who flies an aircraft.

propeller – a set of blades that spin and help an airplane fly.

radar – a system that locates things by bouncing radio waves off them.

reconnaissance – a mission for gathering information.

rotor – a set of blades that spin and help a helicopter fly.

sonar – a system that locates things by bouncing sound waves off them.

INDEX

ONLINE RESOURCES
popbooksonline.com

Scan this code* and others like it while you read, or visit the website below to make this book pop!

popbooksonline.com/military-aircraft

*Scanning QR codes requires a web-enabled smart device with a QR code reader app and a camera.